Parent's Guide to School

Dr. Sophia Crawford-Mapp

Parent's Guide to School

A guide to navigating the process with support

Dr. Sophia Crawford- Mapp

Sophia Latrell Publishing

Sophia Latrell
Publishing

ISBN
978-1-7349679-1-3

Printed in the United States of America

Author's page

Who am I? Good Question….

I am a Woman of God that lives by the scripture 1 Thessalonians 5:16-18.

I am a Wife to a wonderful husband & dad; Love you Anthony (smiles), Dion!

I am a Mom with two awesome, extremely different kids, Carter & Ava.

I am an Educator with 16 years of experience in grade pre-k- 8th grade. #Lexington2SC #UnionCountyNC #CharMeckCountyNC

I am an Advocate that wants to know better in order to do better.

I am Dr. Sophia Latrell Davis Crawford Mapp! There is a story and educational journey behind all 6 of those names that define who I am.

I started school at 3 years old and completed the journey at 36 with a Doctorate!
#MarionCountySchoolsSC #PresbyterianCollege #ColumbiaCollege #WIngateUniversity #ConverseCollege #GardnerWebbUniversity

dr.slmapp@gmail.com

Parent's Guide to Starting School

Dedication

First to God be the glory!

Second to Parents who are navigating this school process for the ones they love the most, the children.

Third to my family all 26 aunts and uncles and all of their offspring! Yes, my granddaddy was busy, Cleveland Adams Sr.

Fourth to my family that I draw experiences and knowledge.

Fifth to Woman Who War that birthed the writing spirit within me.

Crawford-Mapp

Table of content

Introduction

Have you ever wondered if I am doing
this school thing right? Should I be
doing more for my child? Am I asking
too little or too much from my child?
Why is school so different? If you have
asked yourself this, this book is for you.
I have a unique point of view. I am an
educator that became a parent so I have
two viewpoints to pull from.

School was easy to navigate through
and work in but that all changed once I
had to start thinking about where to
send my baby. I started thinking about
am I teaching as hard as I want my
babies teacher to teach and am I
answering all the questions for parents
that they know to ask and more based
upon what I would ask.

This book comes from a place of
knowledge seeking for me. I wanted to
make sure I asked all the questions and

navigate through the school system to make sure my baby was getting what he needs and me not getting fired. I am a little special when it comes to my son and his education as a brown male.

I am fortunate that I can choose to send my baby anywhere in the school district that I could drive. One of the few perks of being an educator. To make the process even more confusing and hair greying; my husband works for a different school system so now we have twice the options as other parents. Let me add that we did not consider any private school options because I believe school should have me changing my lifestyle. Also, we did not consider charter schools because I just didn't know enough about them and I didn't want to add more to my plate of things to do. Picking the right fit, will be another book because that is a whole different process.

I am writing this book because I want to provide parents and guardians with a toolkit of knowledge to make sure they are putting their child first.

The school

The place where your child is 8 hours a day, 5 days a week is a big deal. As a parent, I want better for my child than I had, and this requires work on my part.

Many people are tied to a school because of where you live. You may be in a particular neighborhood because you grew up there, it's a family tradition, it's zoned for "the best" school or you just moved to town and this seller or renter said yes first. Regardless of the reason it's still important to think will this school meet my child's academic and behavioral needs. YES, you need to look at both of these things.

Let's use my love, Carter for example. Background. I picked the house I live in because it had a nice yard that he could play in. It is in the outskirts of town because I am an introvert and don't want to "people" all the time; this process limited my school choices. I work on one side of town and refuse to be in traffic for hours; this limited my school choices even more. I am a no-nonsense mom and will tighten my baby up if he doesn't have respect to the level I want; this limited my school choices even more. Carter was above level entering school; this limited my school choices even more. Carter loves math and science, so I want to put him at a school that emphasized this; this limited my school choices even more. I went from the choice of 135 to 5 elementary school choices in my district. That's a big difference.

Questions to ask yourself about the school you picked, or your child is zoned for.

1. What's the school focus?
2. How many of the teachers have credentials?
3. What is the turnover rate of teachers and staff?
4. Are they certified in the area they are teaching?
5. Are they stern or fluffy?
6. How many classes are there per grade level?
7. What's the daily schedule?
8. Do they offer before or after school?
9. What's the discipline process?
10. What is the school's letter grade?
11. Did they make expected academic growth?

You need to know if the school has an additional focus beyond the basics. The basic focus is to educate all students. Is the school a STEM, STEAM, Technology, Language school? You

want to make sure it matches your
child's needs because it guides the
success of the child. Let's say the
school has a math focus and you know
your child loves the ARTS. You child
could very well be successful but are
you helping to cultivate your child's
strengths and interests. Your child will
begin to think and shift learning focus in
middle school and you want to help start
creating interest for careers. Does the
school stress the use of technology?
This is key because homework and
projects will have a technology
component. You will need to have a
computer with printing options. You will
have to print homework when it's lost,
review the teacher webpage because
your child forgot what they are
supposed to do on an assignment and
you accidently threw away the sheet
because it was left on the kitchen table.
Does the school have a language
focus? This is key because your child
will have to become proficient in another

Crawford-Mapp

language and you will have to help with assignments, and you may not know any Mandarin or French?

Did you know all teachers don't have a teacher's license? Did you know that a teacher has 3 years to gain their credentials? Is your child in that class? Which may not be a big deal to you, but can you do 8th grade math. Do you know what a punnett square is? Is a long-term sub in your child's class as the teacher? Did you know in order to be a substitute all you need is a high school diploma? You know someone that you graduated with that you laugh every time you hear their name. Now picture that person teaching your babies class. How many open positions are in the school? Open positions equal substitutes or larger class sizes. The class size was supposed to be 25 now 2 teachers on the grade level are out and now class size is 32. Now picture 1 teacher with 32 kindergarten kids.

Why is turnover important? You need to
know why teachers are leaving. Did
they retire, yay for them and best
wishes. Did they leave mid-year
because of the workload? Are the
students or parents running teachers out
of the profession? Did they leave
because the reality of their paycheck
kicked in? Is the majority of the staff
new? New teachers need mentors to
help them be successful with academics
and behavior needs in their class. If
there are more new teachers than
veterans, the veterans are going to be
overworked because mentoring a
teacher is a minimum of 1 meeting with
the new teacher per week. The WHY is
important so ask don't assume or claim
ignorance because your child's
education (success or failure) is on the
line and it is a direct result of your level
of questioning.

Are teachers fluffy or stern? Do you have a warm and fuzzy kid that loves hugs and talking, and the teacher doesn't want to get kid germs? Does your kid love to talk and the teacher only fosters academic language and your kid can only talk during lunch and recess/break time? Kids need an outlet and if movement and conversation is not fostered and requested how will your child's language skills grow? Can you imagine sitting still for an hour without talking and moving and you are not watching a movie or asleep?

How many classes are on the grade level? If you are at a small school and your child has a concern with one teacher and the other teachers' class is full, where does your child go? Are you going to ask your child to be placed in a full class and now the teacher is resentful to you, your child and the other teacher who is getting paid the same things as her with less kids?

Parent's Guide to Starting School

That was a lot of food for thought, now let's break it all down to help give you tools to navigate through school and a few sample questions to ask.

Choosing a school

To determine which school your child will go to, you will need to do an address search. Every school district has some type of portal to type in your address and determine which school your child will go to. If you are not technology savvy that is ok, you will have to call the school district and ask for student placement and they can support you with this. This is the avenue I would try first because it will give you a correct answer immediately. With the speed of school districts changing and rezoning you may not want to ask your neighbor because there are some neighbors that are divided, and the left side of the road attends one school and the right side goes to a different school. Don't assume that the closest school to your house is the one your child would attend. For example, we can walk about 2 miles and get to a school and this is not the school that my children are zoned for. Please don't assume, ASK!!

There is a second way to choose a different school other than the one that is attached to your physical address. This option can be called a lot of things such as lottery, magnet, choice, etc. Regardless of what it is called it consists of a process and depends upon the school system. One major thing to know is that you need to start looking into the process around November before the following school year starts. Yes, I know this seems like a long time but if you are in a school with a lottery process this could be deemed as a little late. This option has to be completed through the district office.

My lottery example,
I wanted to enroll my daughter into preschool and we almost did not get in the
lottery. The first round of the lottery is
typically when preschools get filled. For
my district, you have to enroll your child
into school first which is about a 10-day
process because the school collects all
the information and then it is sent to the
district office to be processed. Once this
is done the student's username and pin
are mailed to you. After you get this
information then you can complete the
lottery process. During this time also
you have to take your child to complete
a preschool screening.

The third way is to write a letter to
student placement and ask for a change
based on the school's rating. If your
child's homeschool (the school based
on your address) is a failing school you
can request that your child attends a
different school. There are several
factors to consider when thinking about

this choice because you may have to provide transportation yourself. This may seem like no big deal for most but if your attendance becomes an issue you may be asked to leave and return to your homeschool. This option has to be completed through the district office. I have never completed this process, but I am going to draft a letter that I would write.

Example. Dear Student Placement. My name is Sophia Crawford- Mapp and my son, Carter attends XXX School. Currently this school has a failing rating and they have had this rating for the past 2 years. I am requesting that my son's school placement be changed from XXX to XXX school. I believe that this current placement is hindering his ability to perform at his full potential. Currently the school is performing at 23% proficient. This means that only 6 students per class is proficient and with this current level. I feel that there is no way that the teacher can provide this level of differentiation within each class. Currently my son is one of the 6 proficient students. In addition to academic concerns, I am also concerned with the behavior issues that are currently taking place within the school. My son reports weekly of negative behaviors that negatively impact class instruction and impede it from being successful.

Thank you for reading and considering my request. I look forward to hearing from you soon. My email address is XXX and my phone number is XXXX.

Let's unpack this letter because there are data points that you will need to enter to make your letter pack a punch. 1. You need to know the school rating. You can get this from two places. If you are in NC you can go to the school's web page or you can go to the following website https://www.dpi.nc.gov/data-

<u>reports/school-report-cards</u> and look up your school or call the school and ask the staff members. The teachers, assistant principals and principal will have this score. 2. You need to know how long the school has had this rating and you can get this information from the same sources listed in number one. 3. You will need to know the actual proficiency number, and this could be found in the same place. 4. You will need to know about discipline level, and you can get this by asking the assistant principal and principal. I am going to preface this by saying they will probably be guarded by this information but ask for generalizations such as how many incidents do you have a day or week in 5th grade.

The fourth way you can possibly change school is based upon your living situation. If you are homeless (you don't have an address) you can file for a McKinney- Vento status. There are

Crawford-Mapp

legal documents that you will have to complete and the person you are staying with has to complete documents as well. This is an option that can happen at most schools.

Daily schedule

There are several components to think about when preparing your child for success each day in class. When thinking about a school, grade level or class schedule you need to think about your kid. You need to compare your child's current schedule to the one they are going to have. Yes, kids adjust daily but there are ways to prepare your child for success with this transition. Think about the following: What time does the school day start and what time do you have to be at work?

My example. Currently I have to be at work at 8:30 am and my son can arrive at school between 7:30- 8:00am so this schedule works for me in the morning. He gets out of school at 3:00pm but I don't get off work until 4:30 so I enrolled him in an afterschool program. He has to be picked up before 6:00pm. Yes, this is a long day but it works for us. He gets his homework done in afterschool and he gets some extra socialization time which is huge because we don't live near kids.

Also, think about the amount of travel time in the morning and in the afternoon. Can you effectively drop your kid off at school and make it to work in time? Luckily, I have a 10-minute ride without traffic from his school to mine and a 20 minute ride with traffic.

Are you going to put your child on the school bus? What time does the school bus arrive? What is the route the bus is going to take? How old is your child because there are no seat belts on a school bus? Can your child sit down that long without getting out of their seat?

Also, when you are thinking about schedules think about your child's perceived or noted areas of strengths

and concern.   What do I mean by this?
My son loves math and science but
doesn't care for reading. Yes, this
breaks my heart because reading is the
gateway to school success. I am
fortunate this year that he has reading
class first block while he is fresh. Last
year this wasn't the case and boy could
we tell because every afternoon ride
home talked about his dislike for
reading.

You have little control over which class
your child is placed but this would be a
good thing to include in the all about my
kid letter that you are going to share
with the new principal of your child's
school. Yes, you need to write a letter
because your child is more than a score.
If you start with the school in elementary
school, they know a little about your kid
because there is a kindergarten
placement test so they can see your
kids as a whole child. In middle school,
the first thing they see is a score for

your child to include End of Grade (EOG) scores, report card grades and the discipline record. This may be good or bad, but it doesn't share what makes your kid tick. I will share our letter example. I am not saying this is a perfect letter, but this is one for our son.

Dear Principal

My name is Sophia and I am the parent of a new third grader coming to your school. We are transferring from XXX to your school.   I have heard of the care that you take to get to know all students and the thought and effort you put into matching students with teachers to meet their academic and social/ emotional needs. We received recommendations from parents that are in our Cub Scout troop. Since Carter is new to your school, I would like to share a little about him. He is a well-behaved student and he will NOT be a behavior concern. I am not saying my child is perfect by any means, but we do not tolerate misbehavior at school of any kind. If anything happens to arise, I am only 10 minutes away. He loves math and science. He enjoys attempting to solve math in his head and he loves rocks. I know rocks are covered in science in depth next year. He does not care for reading at much. He can read but struggles with solving multi-syllabic words in the moment (while reading a paragraph or longer text). He will skip the word and keep going. He has attention concerns and we are sampling medication for anxiety and focus (he is not hyperactive). I will keep you guys abreast of any potential side effects so you guys can support him and us with this. He will not take medication at school right now. He is not thrilled about changing schools, but this is a decision we made based upon changes that are going to happen with his current school. He is concerned with making friends, but he does know three other

Crawford-Mapp

boys that attend your school. I feel he would benefit from a teacher that is stern but doesn't yell because he will cry when someone yells at him because it will take it personal. He will need someone that will say what they mean and mean what they say. I would love for him to have a teacher with high expectations to help instill in him that she/he believes he is capable of achieving greatness. I know you will make the best decision for him and us. Thanks for taking the time to read our letter.

Electives

Electives are typically classes other than reading, writing, math, science or social studies such as art, music, physical education, computer, etc. Each school treats the elective schedule differently and the electives that are offered at each school is dependent upon the school.   This could be based on if the school has a speciality such as language immersion, STEM/ STEAM, talent development, etc. It also depends on what side of town your school is on. This also depends on the size of the school because the larger the school the more teachers will be allotted to support the elective teacher team.

In some elementary schools, students visit one class a day and a different class each day of the week. This is also dependent upon the size of the school and the number of electives they offer at each school. If there are five electives, they can go to one per day for a week or if there are only four a school may have a class double up on one. Electives are the time that teachers get to plan and have a break from the lovely kiddos.

Electives in Middle and High School are different because students typically pick their classes depending upon the number of electives offered. A kid will typically have the same two classes (one for A day and a different one for a B day) for a semester and then change to a different one.

This is important because what if your kid hates art and his day begins with art every Monday. What tone is this setting for his day and week. What if your kid starts with PE and forgot to put on deodorant?

If you move or enroll in a school over the summer, you would want to ask to be in contact with the school counselor or master scheduler because you want to have some say in these classes. This will also help your child have a little control of their day because they got to pick a class versus being placed in them. In middle and high schools, students are placed in classes based on their achievement level.

Crawford-Mapp

Breakfast/ Lunch

Please don't think that all food is created equal especially if you jump through hoops with food at home or if you cook more than one meal to appease everyone in your house.

When will the children eat lunch, someone in the school has to be last or first? Does the first group eat at 10:30 or the last group at 1:30? What time do you feed your child? What are you going to pack for lunch? Is your child a picky eater? Have you reviewed a school's lunch menu? Does your child eat anything that they cook? I have a picky eater and I found out this the hard way. He was starving after school. It wasn't until I started digging and asking what you ate today and I discovered he wasn't eating. No one at school contacted me and said your child doesn't eat at school. Of course, I was a little extra that I emailed the teacher. I discovered that teachers had duty free lunch and the lunch monitors rotated and they typically didn't know students' names. Packing lunch is not as simple as one would think. You have to have food that doesn't require warming and at the school Carter is at if you have anything with nuts you have to sit at a separate table because several students have peanut allergies. We found out this the hard way because you are socially isolated if you have these items. Do I like it NO? I think that if you have the allergy then you move but this school doesn't work that way. Yes, my kid loves peanut butter and I thought this was going to be a great go to lunch but NOPE. He does not care for cold cuts, so we are struggling. He packs a lunch daily, but I do have money on his lunch account just in case there is something there that he wants to eat.

Crawford-Mapp

School fit is a vital part of your child's education. When I say school fit, I am asking if the school fits your child's interests and needs. Taking the time to see if a school offers classes in things your child is interested in can determine if school will be a choice or not. Also, if your child needs remediation or enrichments does the school have a time built into the schedule to meet your child's academic needs.

Growth

Your child's educational growth should be on your mind often. Students that are above, on or below grade level should always grow. If a teacher understands and notices the subtle details of instruction and curriculum is key. Knowing what skills your child has mastered and the skills that they still need to master will be the key to your child making growth or not. Example. An ELA standard could be to determine the meaning of words and phrases as they are used in a text, including words that affect meaning and tone. You need to ensure your child knows the isolated sections such as words with multiple meanings, idioms when you are reviewing phrases and they need to know tone. A teacher could say that a student doesn't get this standard but as a parent you need to know which section of the standard.

Growth can be measured from quiz to quiz, test to test, benchmark to benchmark as long as you are comparing apples to apples. What I mean is don't let someone (or you) think that he/ she made a 60 on a test and a 75 on a quiz and they are making growth. No Ma'am!

Most schools offer some type of benchmark that includes smaller components. If you are using this to determine growth, please look at the whole picture AS WELL AS each of the smaller components. For example, if you are using the MAP assessment, you will get a reading score but you will also get an informational text, literal text and vocabulary score and when you look at growth you want to look at all four sections. If a teacher doesn't share this then you need to ASK.

Discipline

It is important for you and your child to know and understand the expectations of the school. Most public schools have the same rules and guidelines. To get a little technical, they will be listed in the district's pamphlet and on the website. For the purposes of your child, you need to know the rules of each of the classes they are in. There could be subtle differences, but this can mean the difference between your child enjoying a class or not. Example, as a teacher I want my students to be very independent, so I review rules and expectations thoroughly for the first 2 weeks and revisit them based upon long breaks and getting new students. After this time, I expect students to know the flow and they will have minor redirections and consequences after this. To be a little more specific, I have entry expectations. Students have 3 minutes to complete entry expectations.

Crawford-Mapp

Their voices are on a level 1 while they unpack, gather materials and turn in homework or other assignments. Once the timer goes off, they are in their seat and starting the do now activity. If voices are too loud, they will get a verbal redirection, if they are not unpacked, they will receive a lost point. We use a behavior matrix at my school. If they are out of their seat when the timer goes off and doesn't start, they lose another point and are now on silent lunch. I am a stickler for time, but they may have another teacher who is more laxed expectations your student might not lose any points for the above items. Sometimes the difference in classes can be hard for a student to transition between and other times students are fine. You need to know your child.

Beginning of the year

It is important to start your child off on the right foot. I think it is imperative to attend an open house and purchase your child's school supplies before the first day of school. Open house may be the first time that you meet your child's teachers. Teachers are the ones that are taking care of your child for the majority of their wake hours. This is a time that you can put a face with a name and the teacher can do the same. This is the first impression that the teacher forms of you and vice versa. If you are new to the school this is the first time you can meet administration as well. This is a key if you know your child might be a little mischievous and frequent their office.

School supplies are important to the success of your child's day. As a teacher we do not hoard your child's supplies and yes students go through a ton of supplies in one week. Please know that it is not the teacher's responsibility to provide items for your child. Yes, materials are used on the first day of school. Think about how your child may feel when the class starts with an all about me activity in elementary school or design your notebooks in middle school and your student doesn't have notebooks or colored pencils or crayons to do this activity. What will your child do while others are working? How will they feel because this is a result of parent issues not student? What will your child do once instruction starts, and it is time to take notes and do work? Yes, most teachers will have loose leaf paper and a pencil but is your child organized enough to keep up with these papers?

I believe the way a school year starts are the way the school year will progress. Please don't put your child and teacher in a hard spot because your child is going to feel some type of way and your child's teacher will always because all teachers want students to succeed. If you are in a bind, please reach out to the teacher, guidance counselor or social worker to ask for support.

During the beginning of the year is a time for you to touch base with your child about their agenda. If an agenda is not provided by the school, I would highly recommend that you get one for your child because this can be where they track homework and other assignments to come. You know your child best and you know if they can remember what is given to them as assignments or not. You can ask each afternoon to let me see your agenda and what your assignments are.

Conferences

Each school has a policy on how many conferences teachers are required to have. For example, most schools require all students to have a conference after the first grading period and all others are optional. I would definitely disagree with this policy. I feel that you need to have a conference with all of your students' teachers every grading period. It doesn't matter if your child is passing or not; I feel that there's always room to improve and you won't really know what your child needs to improve on unless you communicate and meet with teachers.

Also, I feel once a student is at least 2nd grade they need to be in the parent teacher conference because it is one thing for you to know what your student needs to work on but it is another for them to know as well. It is also important for them to know that you and the teacher are on the same page and are united in their improvement and growth.

Once a student is in about 4th grade I believe that they need to co-lead or lead the conference. With this being said, I feel that in order for this to work students need to have individual and/ or group conferences and the teacher needs to share what they are doing well and what they are currently working on. At any grade beyond 4th, the student must be an integral part of all conferences. By this point education has shifted from learning to read to reading to learn and students have to want to do better.

Grades

Grades are the way of school and there is no way around it with the current state of education. It doesn't matter what grade your child is in there will be grades. Typically, in lower elementary k-2 students have four grade options 1, 2, 3 and 4. Four means above grade level, 3 is on grade level, 2 is below grade level and 1 is significantly below grade level. These numbers translate loosely to alphabet grades once a student enters third grade. There are two translations for letters to grades based on the number system. The first translation is a grade of an A is equal to a 4, B is a 3, C is a 2 and 1 is a D. The second translation is a grade of an A is equal to a 4, B is a 3, D is a 2 and a F is a 1. The translation depends on the teacher that you are talking to and most will not translate the lower elementary number scale to upper elementary letters because it can be a hard conversation based on the student's grades.

To delve a little deeper with grades, once grades translate into alphabet, it will be part of a student's responsibility to check their grades and request makeup assignments and for remediation of skills not mastered. During this time, it would also be key for students and parents to monitor grades online. Most school districts use a platform called PowerSchool which gives you real time grade updates.

Once a student enters middle school (in some cases) and in high school grades are vital to monitoring if material is mastered or not. This is uber important because the exam (end of course test) will determine if a student gets credit for a class or not. If credit isn't received that will mean the student has to take the class again.

Grades are also important because it could be the difference between your student staying in the same grade or going to the next grade at the end of the year.

Attendance

When I talk about attendance, I am going to reference tardiness and absences because these are both important terms. It is important that your child is at school on time and remains the entire day. Yes, things and life happen but think about the material that is missed. When is your child going to make this up? It is not on a teacher entirely to stress the importance or remind students to make up missed work. I know that may be hard for some to swallow but let's do the math to make this concept a little clearer. A school day is about 7.5 hours long. You have lunch, which is 30 minutes, recess (elementary and middle) which is 30 minutes, electives/ special which are about 1 hour, bathroom breaks 15 minutes, discipline or class interruptions 15 minutes (this is being modest) which leaves 5 hours for instruction. You have

4 main subject areas which gives about 1 hour and 15 minutes per subject area (75 minutes). Each class has about 25 kids in elementary and more in middle and high. You take away 25 minutes for teacher direct instruction. This is when the teacher is teaching the class a concept. That leaves about 2 minutes per child per subject for a student/ teacher conference or instruction.

If your child is late for a class twice a week, they could be missing 2 lessons and based on the pacing of concepts this could be the only time these concepts are reviewed in that grading period. This could also be the case if your child leaves a class early. Think about if your child is absent for 3 days due to a stomach bug which is part of life. Can they make it up? You could be the deciding factor. Are you communicating with teachers to see what is missed?

Parent's Guide to Starting School

Truancy is when your child misses more than 10 days of school and the school can legally take you to court about excessive absences in school. Yes, there are rules about age around this but would you want to miss work to go to court and have a judge put stipulations on your child's attendance and possible penalties for you. I know you may be thinking that out of 180 days of school what is 10 days. It is a big deal because in high school or middle school if your child is taking a high school class, these days can determine if your child has to repeat a class or not because regardless of the grade your child has if they miss 10 days they are required to retake the class.

Crawford-Mapp

Communication

The concept of communication could be
a book all by itself. This is very
important to your child's success in
class and out of class. Once you attend
an open house you need to share all of
your contacts with all of your child's
teachers. Most teachers these days will
have you complete an all about me
sheet and ask for contact information or
have a class google sheet set up for you
to complete your information. If these
systems are not in place, then you as a
parent need to come with or create this
information and share with teachers.
Yes, I mean that you need to write down
your phone numbers (work and cell) and
email address for teachers.

Communication goes a little deeper than
just sharing your information. You need
to communicate with teachers at least

once a month. This could be as simple as an email to say how is Carter doing. Or What does he need to improve upon? Or What can I do at home to support class work? Many schools also use an agenda to communicate back and forth between home and school.

If there is an agenda, this is where students write down homework assignments and this allows for a clear school to home communication of class expectations. Communication is also the student's responsibility as well.

To improve communication as well you could reference the class or school's websites to know what is going on in class and asking your child about what they learned in school and what are their areas of strengths and concern. If something is stated by your child, then you now have talking points and a list of concepts that were taught and covered in class.

Crawford-Mapp

Chain of command

I believe in confronting the source of concern. If there is an issue, please narrow down the focus of your concern to know who to contact. When I speak chain of command, I am thinking from the bottom up and the bottom is your student, then teacher, the assistant administrator, the principal and then the district superintendent and then the news. YES, I mentioned news because there are some things that may need that step but I can't think of many.

Example 1. If there is an issue with a student and your child, please talk to your child about the situation and gain perspective. I always ask my child if he can handle the situation or does, he need me to intervene. If the situation continues, I will email the teacher to gain additional insight because by NO means will I ever think my child is telling me the truth always. If the situation continues, I will ask for a face to face with the teacher because I don't tolerate bullying.

Let me stop right here and clarify my definition of bullying and what it is and is not. A bully is someone that preys on another student. It is not two students picking at each other and one student's feelings are hurt. It is not one student stating a fact and one student not liking it and telling on another. Sorry for the rant but the word bullying is being used in the wrong context from my perspective.

Example 2. If you have an issue with the teacher with instruction or behavior. Please have the conversation with the teacher before you call the district office staff. I would argue that you need to have at least two conversations depending upon the situation. No situation is okay to dance around if safety or mental stability are in question.

There are situations that need for you to skip the chain of command, but I am not talking about these issues. I do believe that there are tiered situations. If your child and another child are feuding this is tier one so talk to the teacher. If your child isn't growing academically this is tier two and you need to talk to the teacher. If you are on a field trip and children's safety is a concern this would be tier three, and you need to talk to administration but have the conversation with the teacher as well. If someone is stealing your child's lunch money, this is tier two-ish and you need to contact the teacher and email the administrators because you may not know the location of the incident and it might not be on the teacher to deal with. By no means am I saying my Tiers are law, but it is just a guide that I use. Yes, the tiers can go up depending on the solution to the lower tiers or if something happens and you need to skip people. You will also skip a few people if the offender is an adult.

Final Thoughts

I truly believe that my days as an educator before kids shaped my parenting because I witnessed and heard about some interesting parenting techniques. During this time, I was a Preschool Special Education Teacher which means I taught three and four year old students with disabilities. I had them in my class for half of a school day and I had two groups that made up my day. I was fortunate at this time to have two of the BEST assistants ever to walk the earth, Cindy Gleaton and Sharon Robinson at CWECC in South Carolina. During this time, I realized that there were four essential components needed in school; consistency, understanding, communication and PATIENCE.

You could definitely see a difference in students whose parents lived by these components and who didn't because it showed up in their students daily.

Consistency has many facets. Consistency with a balanced meal. This showed up because you can tell the students who ate a sugar filled breakfast and crashed two hours later or the students who only had something to drink and are crying because of stomach pains and hunger or those who ate a balanced meal and are ready to go. Consistency with a constant bedtime. You could tell those that slept with the dog (literally and had fleas), those that slept on the floor and are dirty, those that slept with parents and have separation anxiety because mom/ dad is their security blanket or those who are becoming independent and slept by themselves and want to share their victory each day.   Consistency with completing work. Consistency with self- care to include but not limited to bathing, potty training and feeding. You can tell students who can't feed themselves and have to wait for a teacher to help them. Those that never

Crawford-Mapp

learned to use a fork and spoon and have to change after each meal. Or those students that mastered self-feeding and can ask for seconds while others just look on and wait. MOST of all CONSISTENCY with advocating for your child. This is the hardest for educators especially if they aren't secure in their teaching. It is a parent's job to speak up for their kid to include the good, bad and the ugly. All of these variations of consistency are important, but I can't seem to rank order them because they equally have importance. To some and me at first these items seem to be a NO brainer BUT life happens, and I can give a story to why a parent can't provide all of these things.

Understanding is hard to do but vital to the success of school. A teacher may not like some things but understanding the premise behind the action is paramount and the same goes for parenting. It is hard to say and kind of

Parent's Guide to Starting School

hypocritical but there are times when it is okay to break the rules but if you never "dig a little deeper" you will only see the one side to the three-sided story.

Situation 1- A (three year old) student comes to school with deep scratches down the side of their neck. As an educator you are a mandated reporter for any signs of abuse. You ask the student what happened and they say "mom scratched me". What do you do? HMMMM! Choice1- call DSS and report it, yes this is a fair choice. Choice 2- call mom and say what happened to Dion? Definitely. Choice 3- You do choice 1 and Choice 2. I did choice 3 because I like my job. Come to find out Dion took off running from mom and mom reached out to grab him because a car was coming and the first thing, she could grab was his shirt and she scratched up his neck. There was a note in his bag, but I didn't get that far with a note from the Doctor because she

took him to get checked out. I told mom
that I called DSS and explained my
situation.

Situation 2- A student came to school
daily without getting their agenda signed
and mom never responded to any notes
that I wrote. As a teacher I asked, did
you show this to mom and the student
said yes faithfully. As usual, I would call
mom and share my thoughts and then
move on. After a few weeks of this I am
thinking why this lady isn't responding to
me in this lovely communication folder
that I created, hahaha! By this time, I am
chatting with others and trying to figure
out what in the devil is going on. I am
torn, do I stop writing in the folder or
what because it is not like I have tons of
time on my hand and have nothing else
to do. So, I decided to call because
assuming was getting the best of me.
Mom couldn't read in cursive, so I
switched to print and things improved. I
told her that I wrote in cursive because

my handwriting was horrible and cursive hid it a little.

The point of these situations was to share that you need to judge, criticize less and take an extra minute to figure out the root cause of the situation.

A parent's schedule is like a 500-piece puzzle with no picture to guide you. I am only going to speak to my schedule shifts because that's all I know. I had three major school schedules in my life: single, single mom and married mom with two kids. Help me Lord! I don't know if I can say one was truly easier than the other, but each had its ups and downs.

Single life
As a single person it was initially hard for me to understand a parent's perspective. I had "free" time to get my work done and have a personal life, yet I am not that naive to think that parenting

works the same because I have nieces, nephews and cousins. But yes, there is a BUT, I am the mean one in the family and I don't like to repeat myself and I will tear your butt up if you tried it. Yes, I am old- school and country. I believed in systems and structures that needed to be in place to be effective and this was instilled in me daily as a kid. I grew up in the era of don't interrupt other adults, stay out of adult business and stay in a child's place. I was not privy to adult business.

I had a schedule for my Monday to Friday life. There was a set time to wake up, get out of bed, get dressed, eat, leave the house, travel to work, work, leave work, get home, cook, do school work, watch my shows, shower and bed. Of course, I fiddled with time to optimize get the right amount of sleep, what not to watch before bed so I would go to sleep and not stay up too late.

Parent's Guide to Starting School

Just as I had a schedule for me, there needs to be a schedule for kids and yes parents you need to find the sweet spots for kids as well. Doctors make suggestions about whether a kid needs 8-10 hours of sleep, is your kid a 8, 9, 10 or 11 hour kid because yes all kids are different. I do suggest playing with the times but not every day and don't jump from 11 to 8 because that will mess with your mood something fierce.

Single Mom
You need to throw all that other stuff out the window and put it all on steroids at the same time. Caring for a tiny person is exhausting!!! At this point my job shifted, my location shifted, and I am further away from family. What in the DEVIL was I thinking? Yes, I had a Monday to Friday schedule but now you have to add time in for another person so there were now alarms for everything. Adding drive time to and

from daycare decreased my sleep time and BOY that was an adjustment. I lived 35 minutes from daycare without traffic and daycare was 40 minutes from work. Yes, you may be thinking of changing daycares, NOPE! I found comfort in knowing Carter was taken care of so who needs sleep and I loved who I worked for, Dr. Kevin Plue (UCPS). Being a single mom, things are unknown, so peace of mind is everything.

Fast forward a few years and scheduling becomes a beast. Now I feel that I need to put the kid in sports so there goes Thursdays and Saturdays. It doesn't just take up time but now this impact eating, now we are eating fast food every week and spending extra money.

Married
Phew, Balance! Yeah right! My husband works 45 minutes from home, and I work 15 minutes from home but when

you add kids to the mix add 15 minutes to each person's one-way trip. Did I mention we live in Charlotte, so we have a little traffic, ugh! One would think that's not too bad but factor in different work schedules, he has an 8-4:30, I have an 8:30-5, and kids have an 8-3 with afterschool. One kid has ballet, one kid has scouts, and both have swimming. Sometime in between we are to be a family and enjoy each other's company. As you can tell we are still trying to find a balance. Could we do more, yes but we are tired!

Regardless of your situation, if you choose to have kids please know that you are the example for them to follow. The things you say and do will always be watching and scrutinized and ingrained in them for life. I do believe children are a product of their environment and it shapes them to be who they are. It will either teach them this is normal, and this is what I need to

Crawford-Mapp

do, or it will be an experience for them to learn upon. The way they deal with it is totally dependent upon the child. I have 3 other siblings and we dealt with the situations in our life completely differently.